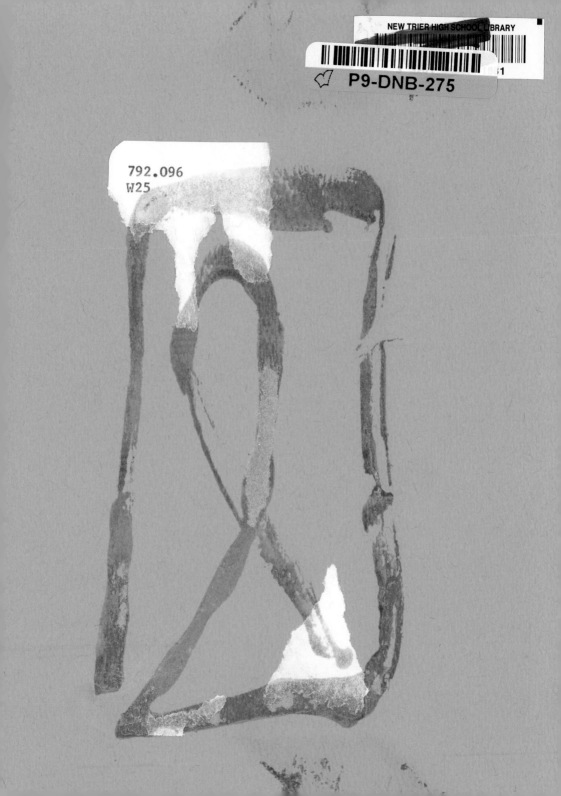

# The
# Theater
# of
# Africa

# THE
# THEATER
# OF
# AFRICA

## AN INTRODUCTION

## Lee Warren

Photographs by

**Judith Bernstein**

Prentice-Hall, Inc. | Englewood Cliffs | New Jersey

Printed in the United States of America    •J

Prentice-Hall International, Inc., London
Prentice-Hall of Australia, Pty. Ltd.,
North Sydney
Prentice-Hall of Canada, Ltd., Toronto
Prentice-Hall of India Private Ltd., New Delhi
Prentice-Hall of Japan, Inc., Tokyo

Library of Congress Cataloging in Publication
Data

Warren, Lee.
   The drama of Africa.

   SUMMARY:   An introduction to modern
drama in the various regions of Africa—its
production, stages, actors, costumes, major
playwrights, etc.
   1.   Theater—Africa—Juvenile literature.
[1.   Theater—Africa]   I.   Title.
PN2969.W3          792′.096          74-20728
ISBN  0-13-219002-2

"Woyengi" from THE IMPRISONMENT OF OBA-
TALA AND OTHER PLAYS by Obotunde Ijimere
reprinted with permission by Heinemann Educational
Books, Ltd., London.

THE PALMWINE DRINKARD is reprinted with
permission of Robert G. Armstrong.

The author would like to thank Judith Bernstein for
her help in researching this volume.

For Beverly and Merritt Kimball
Who made a home for me in West Africa.

# Contents

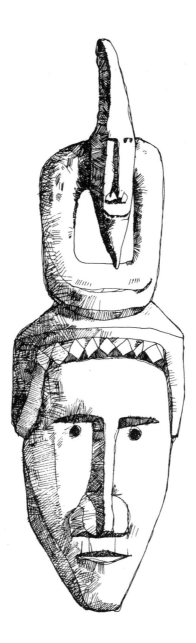

# FOREWORD

In Africa today all forms of drama, past and present, ritual and ceremony, dance mime and modern play, exist side by side. Throughout the continent we find traditional drama in the villages and imported amusements in films and television. Steeped in religion, shaped by folklore and mythology, African drama mirrors the total African experience. European playwrights are as much reflected in the theater of Africa today as are the dramatic play of ritual and ceremony.

Traditional African drama is so integrated into African religions and customs, and music and dance so closely woven throughout, it is unrealistic to define "theater" as a separate cultural entity. In this Introduction we will discuss not only the written plays but all other forms of "staged theater" in Africa, including storytelling, puppetry and ritual drama. In traditional African life, ritual drama embodies all the requisites of theater as Westerners know them—actors, plots, dialogue, rehearsals, props, costumes and makeup.

The arrival of Christian missionary groups in the nineteenth century saw the development of the folk operas, which were based on the entertainment in the churches. Traveling groups of actors performed these operas on tours throughout Africa. Guitar bands known as concert parties brought still another form of theatrical entertainment to remote villages.

Theater in the cities, however, is primarily concerned with drama of a more intense nature, such as the conflict of opposing cultures. A major proportion of black theater in South Africa deals with sketches of urban life and the inevitable corruption of morals. A typical plot incorporates the feelings of the workers toward the boss. Performed in pidgin English, these plays are full of satire, with a frame of reference not understood by outsiders.

Heavy censorship has had its deadening effect on dramatic activity in South Africa. Oppressive laws governing theater attendance deny whites the opportunity to see plays performed by black companies. Since blacks cannot perform in the urban theater halls, the whites do not know what black theater is.

Censorship, however, is not isolated to the Republic of South Africa. Lewis Nkosi, expatriate South African playwright now living in London, told me of the Ethiopian writer doing an adaptation of *Julius Caesar*, who was instructed to amend the plot so that it was Brutus who was assassinated, not Caesar.

Landlocked in his own country, Afrikaaner Athol Fugard of South Africa continues to signal to the outside world the desperate condition of a system that dehumanizes a large group of its people. His plays, *The Blood Knot* and *Boesman and Lena*, are serious indictments of apartheid (the policy segregating the races). Fugard is director of The Serpent Players, a group based in Port Elizabeth, which continues to survive in spite of endless government harrassment.

East Africa struggles with a European imposition not as corrosive as South Africa's racist poison, yet restrictive in another way. So successful were the colonists in this part of the continent that only recently efforts to produce African theater for African audiences have begun to be made.

Today, Africans are discovering and preserving their past at the same time that they are being considerably influenced by what is happening in theater throughout the world. In the same quarter century Wole Soyinka wrote *Madmen and Specialists*, a sophisticated theater piece on a universal theme of the triumph of greed and human expendability, while Duro Ladipo created his classic folk opera, *Oba Koso*, a poetic drama containing traditional praise songs and prayers and a drum orchestra.

But it is in West Africa where the greatest theatrical activity is flourishing. The university departments of drama in Nigeria, Ghana and Ivory Coast, the Arts Council in Accra and the television industry in Nigeria are producing an amazing variety of theatrical forms.

African drama in European terms is young. Yet African drama is old, deeply rooted in the lives of its people and in the memory of the old storyteller who took his place at the end of the workday while the drums called the people together for storytelling time.

# Storytelling

"**A**lmost every African brought up in a village as I was," E. A. Yirenkyi said, "is a good storyteller. This is because right from infancy the old man gets you around the fire and tells you some of his folk stories. You are not conscious of the learning process. You think you are just listening to stories, but by the time you are five or six you are beginning to tell some of the same stories yourself. Although we retell the ones our grandfathers told us, gradually we invent small changes. And by the time a boy is seventeen or eighteen, he is such a beautiful storyteller that if he had the talent to put it all down he would be considered a very good writer."

E. A. Yirenkyi is a professor of drama at the University of Ghana at Legon. Although he represents the modern African markedly influenced by Western academic training and ideas, he is still an African. Like a great majority of Africans whose life begins in the village, his ties to the village life of his childhood are strong and vital. It is this unbroken continuity that distinguishes African theater, a theater deeply rooted in traditional African life of which storytelling is an essential part.

The event of storytelling satisfies the definition of theater, which demands actors, a place to perform and an audience. In traditional African communities storytelling provides both entertainment and moral instruction. It is one of the methods of educating young people by introducing them to the culture, customs and philosophies of their people. Storytelling moves through the rhythm of African life, as a time of shared experience, response and stimulus between the narrator and his audience.

"One day, God said," the storyteller may begin, or he might say, "A story is coming," or "We do not really mean that what we are going to say is true." However he may start, his telling the story is a continuation of the living oral tradition of village storytelling, something non-Africans tend to associate with a "primitive" era that has been swept away by the modernizing effect of Western culture. The reality of modern Africa, however, is that its modern gloss barely covers an enduring core of rural traditionalism. Modern innovations touch gently on the African consciousness.

Narration, acting, drumming and song are all part of storytelling. In the evenings (and *only* in the evenings) the villagers gather in a circle around the fire; the drummers sit behind the storyteller and the children sit to either side.

In traditional order first come the riddles, often designed to teach boys and girls to observe objects in their surroundings.

"He's very short and he has a flat head," the old man says. "What is it?" And a child will answer back, "Nail." Or, "He's very short and he's got a very thick skull," to which the correct response will be, "It's a palm nut kernel."

Perhaps the riddle is, "There are two sons born of the same mother. They want to go to farm but each of them refuses either to lead or keep back. What is it?" The answer is "Feet." "A long thin whip touches both the sky and earth. What is it?" "Rain," the child responds.

Riddles are often in the form of statements even though answers are required. For example, "Elephant dies, Jamu-Jamu eats him; cow dies, Jamu-Jamu eats him." The answer is "Jamu-Jamu dies, there is no one who eats him." Riddles are also an essential element in cultural orientation and moral training. A Yoruba riddle such as "Who is it that goes down the street without greeting the king?" reminds children that when they walk by the king's palace they must go in and greet him.

The first stories of the evening are simple and short, sometimes told by the children themselves, expanding on the tales they know, usually ingenuous reasons for the actions and cries of animals—why the cock crows, why the frog croaks, why the goat stamps the ground. Questions are asked about the origin of natural objects, the justification for the community's ethical code. And then the listeners are told in the summing up:

"That is why Ananse (the spider) is frequently seen against the ceiling. Long ago he used to walk on the ground like the crab." Or, "That is why the tail and chin of the black colobus monkey became white; formerly they were black." "That is why the Babadua reed has knots on its stalk. Formerly the stalk was quite smooth." "That is why the African crow is black all over but has a white band around its neck." "That is why grass dies but rises from the dead, but men die and do not spring forth again." And so on. After the children have played their part, the elders contribute their own tales. Anyone may volunteer to begin with "My story, listen!

14

"Once upon a time there was a big homestead near the hill in which there were many children. One day when all the grown-ups had gone to the field and the old nurse, their grandmother, had fallen asleep in the shades of the big millet granary, the five-eyed Obibi appeared. His teeth were rotten, black as soot, his eyes red as ochre, like the eyes of an opium smoker. His large flapping ears hung loosely, touching his shoulders. A huge bag swung from his long skinny neck, and he held a crooked walking staff in his hand, his claws were long and sharp.

"The children fled in terror. 'Akoo! Akoo!' the Obibi croaked in his ugly voice, saliva dripping from his smelly mouth. 'Come back to me. Do not run away from your grandpa! Come back to me and I will give you some roasted and salted ground nuts mixed with simsim.' Some of the children began to return and then he gave them some roasted and salted nuts. Soon all the children gathered around the Obibi and he gave them all some food, which they ate and enjoyed very much.

"Then the Obibi took out a long rope from his cowskin bag. 'Akoo! Akoo!' he croaked again. 'My grandchildren, let us have a game of tug-of-war.' And the children eagerly agreed. Then he tied one end of the rope around his large testicles, letting it hang loosely behind him, and the children took the other end and began to pull. And as they pulled they sang."

The audience joins in the song. The children gathered around the fire sing the first line and some of the older people sing the chorus, the part of the Obibi. After a while the storyteller continues:

"The children pulled and pulled and danced and danced. Obibi warned them not to tell their parents about his visit or else he would not come again and bring roasted and salted ground nuts mixed with simsim and never again play tug-of-war. The children promised, and the Obibi vanished.

"When the grown-ups came back from the field and asked about the large footprints all over the compound, the children said they did not know. Next day Obibi returned, gave the children more food and again played tug-of-war. But this time he enticed the children away, put them all in his cowskin bag and when he arrived home ate each of them, alive and raw, one after the other until he finished them all."

The moral of the story is clear: Beware of strangers; show more loyalty to your parents than to a stranger.

The traditional stories also include legends about tribal heroes and their military exploits, magical prowess, singular economic fortunes, feats of strength, skill or wit. In African cultures the legends embody the main historic records of the people's past and form an essential part of communal religious celebrations as well.

From Senegal to Mozambique the stories of Africa tell of animals behaving like human beings: the elephant is clever, but shortsighted, impulsive, easily stumbling into trouble; the hyena is a coward; the hare and the spider are incorrigible tricksters. Kwaku Ananse, "spider born on a Wednesday," is Ghana's infamous hero of countless tales.

While all the characters are fictitious and any resemblance to persons living or dead is purely accidental, the morals of the tales are explicit guidelines for responsible, socially acceptable behavior: "Honesty is the best policy." "Pride destroys both body and soul." Their nationally recognized counterparts are found in every ethnic body of folklore, a cliché of the human condition.

The African style of storytelling is a composite of several skills of the teller himself as he recreates his characters, impersonates all of them and fills in the background, describes the scene and builds the plot. With gestures, facial expressions and varying intonations of voice he can create a patterned fabric embodying all of the story's moods and tensions.

Speech is used not only for setting the scene and recounting chronological events but also for commentary. When a bird cries, the teller does not only say that the bird cries, he *makes* it cry in the story. When someone dies, and people mourn, the dirge in progress is *voiced*. The cries of birds and animals, the sound of dripping water, flowing rivers or falling trees may be represented as much as the words of the human and animal characters in the tale itself.

The story belongs to the community in its outline; its text is public property until an individual whose turn it is to tell a story picks it up. Then it becomes *his* story. There is, therefore, no single authentic text. The effectiveness of the tale depends solely on the creative scope of the teller, his movements and voice modulation. A textural comparison between different versions is impossible.

The audience is seldom passive. Listeners will join the storyteller by acting out the narrative. Somewhere in the audience there may be someone who knows a song that fits a part of the story. He can stop the storyteller with a cue, "Hold on to your story—I was there that day," and the storyteller will understand that someone wants to sing a song. The man will perform his song in the acting area, then return to his place.

Action and audience are so intermeshed in the spontaneity of the performance that it is often difficult to identify them as separate entities. Sometimes at a point in the telling, a group will come into the acting area, singing and clapping, accompanied by the drummers, with the audience serving as chorus. This interlude is much like the intermission at Western/European theater, often a necessary comic relief to a more serious and moralistic tale.

In Western terminology, storytelling is whole theater because of its components of narration, acting, drumming and song. Although this type of theater has existed in African society for a long time, it is only recently being viewed as an art form and must, therefore, be labeled appropriately.

Oral village storytelling is a commonplace event for the great majority of Africans who live relatively insulated from urbanization, industrialism and mass communication media. They still enjoy a considerable measure of leisure and stability, and traditional folktales remain an essential part of their social life. For them folk beliefs are valid, and folktales remain an essential element in their education and recreational life.

For the African brought up in the village, the tales are unforgettable, as much a part of his childhood as his family, his friends and the lessons learned around the fire from the old man.

Performance (by the Midwest State at the 1972 All Nigeria Festival of the Arts at Kadunah) of "Everyman" by Wole Ogunyemi

Performance of the Actor's Studio in Accra, Ghana, of "Song of a Goat" by Nigerian playwright John Pepper Clark

# Ritual Drama

The elements of theater include dialogue and movement, costuming, mime and music. While one can speak poetically of the drama of the life experience, a literal chronicling of a daily routine scarcely qualifies as drama. Neither does a ritual ceremony which merely makes a request of the gods and spirits. The core of dramatic art is portrayal, interpretation and expression.

As Ola Rotimi, one of modern Nigeria's most important playwrights, put it, "Ritual displays that reveal in their style of presentation, in their purpose and value, evidences of imitation, enlightenment and/or entertainment, can be said to be drama. While the exciting series of abebe dance processions that highlight the seven-day long Edi Festival of Ile-Ife cannot be termed drama, the mock duel scene preceding the festivities *is* drama." Usually performed on the eve of Edi, it involves two traditional chiefs, Obalayan and Obalufe. The former represents forces of peace, the latter of discord. At the end of the duel Obalufe is taken captive; he offers a ransom and is later released. Obalayan bears the ransom to the Oni, lord of the land, who, on receiving it, declares the Edi Festival begun. The action of the duel is symbolic, as well as entertaining.

A dramatization of the myth of the Oba, which has now become a permanent feature of the annual Obatala Festival in Nigeria, satisfies the definition of ritual drama: plot, conflict and suspense, and entertainment. The drama is a pantomime in three acts, representing three myths. First is the myth of creation which claims that after Obatala fulfilled the command of the Almighty God, Olodudumare, to create the earth, Ile-Ife, he then went on to create man. (The legend explains the creation of the misshapen and crippled as the result of Obatala's temporary loss of his faculties after drinking too much palmwine.) The second, the conquest myth, recalls the arrival on Ile-Ife of a band of immigrants, who under a powerful leader believed to be Oduduwa, invaded, settled and colonized the city-state. Several episodes dramatize the third myth, telling first the story of the civil war between the people of the city and their conquerors, then the imprisonment of Obatala and the release.

Neither the ceremony of "outdooring" a baby, with its ritualistic expression of gratitude to the supreme God, nor the exciting, rhythmic dance movements of the Gelede masquerade are drama; they are merely dramatic. In contrast, the I-Njoku elephant ceremony of the Bakwerri peoples of the Cameroon Republic *does* become drama when masquerades—clad in sack, palm fronds, raffia fluffings and headpieces fitted with wooden projections for tusks between which hang long sugarcane stems representing uprooted trees—dance about with the trampling gait of elephants and sometimes make ferocious jabs with their "tusks" at spectators or into the ground.

Strictly speaking, if specific imitation or re-creation of an experience is missing, suspense and conflict absent, or entertainment lacking, the event cannot be legitimately termed drama. Yet much of traditional African ritual and ceremonial activity seems to straddle a rigid definition.

The Onisigu masquerade, described by Segun Olusola, the Nigerian television playwright and producer, is a remarkable example of a play well staged and properly timed, exploiting the imagination of the spectators, and flawless as ritual.

Onisigu was the most powerful of all the masquerades in Imperu, a little Nigerian town on the plains midway between Lagos and Ibadan. Whenever he came out, all the other little gods dispersed into their graves or, if they were caught unaware, sought the nearest shelter behind broken-down walls, inside drain pipes and on top of village trees, hiding from the wrath of Onisigu, "the great masquerade."

His full name was chanted by the host of women worshippers, who followed him as he marched through the main roads of the village, a long black pole slung across his shoulder, sprinkling "divine" water on the stock and on those who sought his blessing.

The scene usually took place in a dilapidated mud wall in the center of the village. It probably had been a dwelling place, but now the roof was almost gone and birds and lizards made their home there. Hundreds of worshippers gathered around the walls. At the zero hour the chief steward made a spirited, expectant yell, "Onisigu-o . . . Onisigu-o . . . Onisigu-o." And the crowd burst out in refrain, "Afe yin t'omi Orun gogo" (The great one who holds back the floods of heaven with his back). Slowly through the wall emerged first the black pole, then the head and then the whole trunk as "the great god" arrived back on earth. The drama of Onisigu makes use of both stage realism and magical dexterity.

Many traditional African festivals are a complex combination of ceremonies. The Olokun Festival, celebrated at the end of May in a small Yoruba town in western Nigeria when the first yams are ready consists of the worship of Oloku (the principal goddess of the town), the new yam festival, homage to the Oba's (the king's) mother, a sacrifice to the Oba's crowns and symbolic wrestling matches.

The cast of characters in this seven-day festival, in which the entire town participates, includes Olokuku, the chief; Aworo, the priest; Oloku; and the principal god worshipped in the town of Okuku.

The first day's events are concerned with collection of the first new yam by the Aworo, which he presents to the Oba. Kola nuts will then be thrown to divine whether the new year will be prosperous.

On the second day the new yams are eaten. Then the Oba and the Aworo go to the priest's own shrine to sacrifice a yam to Oloku. The Aworo returns to the marketplace to light a fire when the Oba appears, scatters it and throws away the burning sticks. This is the signal for the fight: the Oba and the Aworo begin to wrestle, but tradition demands the Oba must win!

There is feasting on akara (bean cakes) on the next three days. The sixth day is devoted to rest, and on the last day a procession of young girls, led by the Oba's daughters, is made through the town to drive out the evil spirits.

Perhaps the most fascinating part of the whole festival and the tantalizing aspect of dramatic emphasis is the wrestling match between the Oba and the Aworo. The people of Okuku do not explain why custom demands that the Oba must always win. Was there once a quarrel between the king and the priest? Did it symbolize the separation of the secular power from the sacred authority? One can only conclude that the people of Okuku have forgotten the true meaning of the rite.

An integral component of drama is, of course, mime. In traditional African life, acts of a mimetic kind occur frequently at funerals. One of the functions of these mimetic performances is to serve as an obituary, a celebration of the achievements of the dead man. In *Death, Property and the Ancestors*, Jack Goody writes that such performances not only reaffirm the solidarity of the living members of the group in the face of death, they also deliberately eliminate the dead man from their midst.

When a member of Ite Odo dies, for example, the Ohafia War Dance is performed, but only by men who have done some unusually brave deed. Their bodies are decorated with yellow paint, white chalk and ground camwood. One man, assisted by two attendants, carries a huge pot. A white cock and skulls are tied to the pot, into which has been placed a young wine palm plant.

The trumpeter blows his horn to invoke the spirits of deceased members and the glee man sings of the deeds of brave men, past and present. The drummer beats to call them each by his name while the singer knocks two flat sticks together. The climax is reached as the pot carrier and his attendants mime the movements that were typical of the brave men whose names were called. When the man just deceased is buried, the playing stops; it is the sign to bid him farewell.

Examples of ritual drama are as endless as the expanse of the continent. Generally speaking, there are two forms of ritual drama organizations: the secular, for a variety of social events such as fattening, coming of age, weddings and funerals, and the sacred, which may also provide amusement but through its rules governing behavior exerts a broad measure of social control.

Essentially the ritual performance is an act of worship, and although the ritual play is not "staged" the whole festival has a form that gives it an artistic pattern. There is procession, a mass movement of people who gather for the festival either as spectators or active participants; music and song furnish the poetic element. Chanting by the chorus in combination with the drumming communicates thought and mood. For the passive spectator the performance is a work of art; for those actively involved there is a spiritual return. In traditional African life, ritual drama embodies all the requisites of theater as Westerners know them—actors, plots, dialogue, rehearsals before performance, props, costumes and makeup. Only the ticket booth, the ushers and the printed programs are missing.

# Puppetry

In Senegal, a procession of puppets with songs and dances marks the great festival of lanterns, a practice similar to the custom of men bearing small statues during the Osiris festival in ancient Egypt. The Yoruba of Nigeria refer to the carved figure of a puppet as Ajolokeloke, "one who dances in air." The Bambaras call their puppet theater Konoudoukili, Birds' Song. In Kano, puppetry is known as Dubbo-Dubbo. The puppets used in Bornu are called dogodogo. They are all progenitors of Punch and Judy, an entertainment in traditional African society that was not restricted to children but was popular with the entire community.

While the strings of modern marionettes are sometimes camouflaged with sprays and special lighting effects, their ability to delight an audience is no less today than generations ago when the dolls of the Aiyelabola Troupe brought noisy approval from the spectators. J. A. Adedeji, professor of drama at Ibadan University, describes puppetry in his study of the beginnings of Yoruba theater in western

Nigeria. Stiff rod puppets, manipulated manually, were held high above the audience. A typical scene would open with the invocation of the bata drum and a chorus chanting,

> "Let him emerge,
> Let him emerge,
> Let Erugale emerge."

When the puppet appears the chorus sings,

> "He has arrived!
> He that dances in the air has arrived.
> Erugale, it's time to dance."

Dramatically speaking, the story line was simplicity itself. Erugale makes his appearance, a mooning, love-sick man longing for a mistress. Suddenly she appears. They meet, express deathless devotion and almost immediately have a violent misunderstanding, followed by the familiar Punch and Judy knocking and pummeling about. Finally the female figure flees from the stage. End of play.

Traditional puppet theater repertoire, however, includes more interesting plots, usually reflecting daily incidents in the life of the people. The puppets of a Bornu puppet show are rag dolls which slip on to the hand like a glove, fingers being inserted into the head of the doll. When preparing for a performance, the puppeteer, the dog-odogoma, plants a stout forked stick in the ground. He places his hyena-skin bag containing the puppets in front of the stick, then sits down behind it and covers both the stick and the bag with his voluminous gown. His head and the forked stick provide support for the tents so formed while he manipulates the puppets through the opening in the gown made for his head. Drummers stand behind the performer and provide music and song during costume changes inside the tent.

The anthropologist, R. E. Ellison, reported that the dogodogoma does the speaking, but it is almost impossible to distinguish the words since they are uttered in a shrill whistle, at a much higher pitch than is typical of the English Punch and Judy performances. The whistle in this case consists of two pieces of ostrich shell, about three quarters of an inch square, bound together with thread. This is half swallowed by the dogodogoma, who declares that to perfect this whistling voice is by far the most difficult part of his craft and requires years of practice. The words of the puppets, being almost unintelligible, are repeated by one of the assistants in attendance.

A typical performance consists of approximately eight short scenes, each about three or four minutes long. Every scene is complete in itself and has no connection with those preceding or following. Although the cast is usually made up of six puppet characters, no more than two, of course, can appear at the same time. The action is highly dramatic. For example, a thief enters a man's house and is just making off with his swag when the wife wakes up and gives the alarm. Up through the tent comes the husband, who gives the thief a sound thrashing.

Another scene might feature a coy Shuwa Arab girl wearing a lovely, long flowing white gown, her hair adorned with cowries. She sings and dances, captivating a married man whose wife suddenly appears and expresses her displeasure by soundly beating him. A neighbor comes along to see what all the noise is about, and soon his curiosity sparks a great fight with the husband, each party wielding a long stick with murderous efficiency.

The colonial influence is often demonstrated, as in an amusing scene in which a village head informs the sarkin bariki—the manager—that the District Officer is coming to stay at the Rest House. He is a most particular D. O. and the Rest House must be well swept and have plenty of wood and water. Dressed completely in white, wearing a white sun helmet, the D. O. arrives and is greeted by the village head with much respect and bowing. Alas, all is not perfect in the Rest House and the sarkin bariki is severely reproved with shrill cries and a long stick.

The materials used to fashion the puppets depend on what is available in the vicinity. The Tiv people in Eastern Nigeria for example, carve two-foot-high characters out of wood, which are then brightly painted and dressed in elaborate costumes. The puppets, representing monsters, witches or some supernatural power, perform from high platforms in large dramatic masquerades. In the eastern part of the continent, puppets are made with a simple rod and string; one end of the rod is placed in a small hole in the ground while a string attached to the other end is connected to the puppet. The puppeteer holds the tip of the rod in his left hand and beats rhythms on the rod with a stick held in his right hand. Sometimes the children participate in the making of the puppets, using sharpened iron-edged palm branches as tools.

Television, radio and films are still luxuries and, in vast stretches of Africa, are totally unknown. The puppet theater remains a valuable vehicle for entertainment and education, a dramatic medium in communal celebrations and part of the storytelling sessions in the evening. Whether the cast of characters numbers two or thirty puppets, the drama is closely interwoven with the routine, events, morals and philosophy of village life.

The dogodogoma in Yerwa, the big native town near Maiduguri, Nigeria, will give a performance on such festive occasions as weddings and appointments to office. A puppet interlude still punctuates the night-long storytelling masquerades in Ngahor village. The program might feature such stories as "The Boa and the Tortoise," "The Whiteman and Didirin" (the Moron) and "Sango, the Miracle Worker." Elaborate puppet theater is very much a part of the dramatic entertainment in Africa, and not especially for children alone.

Performance of a puppet play (based on historical legend) by middle school students in Northern Ghana (Sandema Middle School)

31

# Folk Opera

By the middle of the nineteenth century various European missionary groups had established spheres of influence in many parts of Africa. They seem to have operated on the principle that European civilization and Christianity were synonymous and that membership in a Christian church was a civilizing process. Under this influence there developed "civilized" communities of educated Africans, some of whom entered the missions as schoolteachers, while others joined the civil service. This elite group regarded the church as the fount of prosperity on earth and salvation in the hereafter. As lay readers in the church, this group was also responsible for introducing entertainments such as cantatas, pantomimes and opera, all enacting biblical themes.

In traditional African life music and mime had been the principle components of the storytelling program. The addition of dance, costume and props were basic to ritual dramatic presentations. Folk opera, based on the entertainments in the churches, developed as a combination of all of these—a whole theater made up of music, dance, song, mime, costume, props, lighting effects and staged settings, an African blend of missionary ethic and deeply-rooted indigenous culture.

Historical events and mythology appear in productions of traveling, contemporary folk opera companies. These companies are organized and directed by actor-managers who write the material, compose the music, choreograph the dances, train the actors and perform on stage. The most famous examples of these traveling bands of players are found in West Africa, particularly in Nigeria and specifically the companies of Hubert Ogunde, Kola Ogunmola and Duro Ladipo.

Ogunde is known as the "father of the Yoruba operatic theater." As a member of the Pentecostal Church of the Lord in Lagos he had been asked, in 1943, to use his musical experience gained while serving as a church organist and choirmaster to produce a service of songs for his new church. Church services customarily contained a good deal of drumming and spirited singing and dancing. Ogunde added some drama based on the biblical account of the fall and salvation of mankind, and the result, essentially a devotional service, was definitely professional theater. He called it "The Garden of Eden" and presented it in 1944.

Originally his plays had no text at all and were totally improvised. It was not unusual for an Ogunde play, based on a single plot structure, to be performed differently on successive evenings. Often the dialogue spoken by the actors depended on the suggestions and responsiveness of the audience. Audience participation during an Ogunde performance is a vital part of an Ogunde evening.

A typical Ogunde plot is contained in his play, *Half and Half*. A hunter saw a deer magically change into a woman, discard her skin on the ground and disappear. The hunter took the hide and put it away in a secret place. When the woman returned, looking for the abandoned skin, the hunter approached her. On the promise that he would return her skin, she became his wife. His other wives were unhappy at the beautiful newcomer's presence and made many attempts to find out the origins of the newest wife. The hunter refused to tell them until he was tricked by his wives into drinking so much that he revealed his secret. Whereupon his wives mercilessly taunted him.

Over the years the subject matter of the plays performed by Ogunde's company has run the gamut from *Journey to Heaven*, a play about the Yoruba belief in predestination, to *The Armed Robbery*, a moralistic piece based on Yoruba folklore about a princess who was discontented with the choice of husband selected for her by her father.

Borrowing from the concert party (see next chapter) of Ghana, Ogunde later incorporated saxophone music and a brass band, and changed the opening glee (song) from the traditional pledge to a Western-style curtain raiser. His stories reflected the music-hall show of broad comedic episodes.

Originally the opening glee (which marked the entrance of the performers) was a pledge both to the gods and to the audience, something like the prologue to a play. The traditional glee man committed himself to the owners of the world in a statement on the belief that this world is not our own, that we must pledge ourselves to the vital force that sustains it. "Please accept the task I have assumed," the glee man says, "I give you every respect, I give you every honor. Let me be able to fulfill my mission. The task is that of someone who has come to entertain but in the entertainment I have something to offer you." For example, this is the opening glee to *Yoruba Ronu* (Yoruba Think) by Ogunde:

"The works of this World are the Lord's;
Mankind is his messenger.
The Almighty who has sent me on errand to the World
Says I must grow to old age, says my life must endure,
Says I must prosper and leave a record behind.
I beseech the World not to worry me;
Allow me to deliver the message of my Creator."

*Yoruba Ronu* marked a trend in vernacular drama toward a concern with the popular scene. After its production in 1964, a frank satiric piece decrying the corruption of government, Ogunde's troupe was banned from performing anywhere in Nigeria's Western Region. Directly afterwards, Ogunde staged a reply to the ban from the sanctuary of Lagos, called *O Tito Koro* (The Truth is Bitter).

In later years Ogunde modified the classic opening glee to a more music-hall type of curtain raiser of Cuban music or Highlife and a line of pretty dancing girls.

Three decades after Ogunde's first company was formed, the players are now separated into the Ogunde Theatre Company, Ogunde Dance Company and Ogunde Concert Party. No matter where the companies travel—to Dahomey, Ghana, the United Kingdom, Canada for Expo '67, or the Apollo Theatre in New York City's Harlem—the plays are presented in the vernacular Yoruba.

Kola Ogunmola's death early in 1973 brought a close to the career of a superb actor who was the director and manager of the Ogunmola Traveling Theatre and one of the original members of the renowned Ori Olokun Workshop.

Ogunmola began his professional career, as did Ogunde, as a schoolteacher. In 1948 he organized a group of teachers and students, wrote plays on biblical themes, such as *Nebuchanezzar* (later in 1959 retitled *Reign of the Mighty*) and

35

traveled from place to place putting on performances of folk opera. At first his company performed for no salary, asking only for enough food to sustain them. Transportation from village to village was by foot, with cooking utensils and stage props on their heads. Illumination of the improvised "stage" was by gas lamps held on the heads of two boys at either end of the stage.

Of all the plays offered by Ogunmola's Theatre, the one most closely identified with him is his great work, *The Palmwine Drinkard,* based on the novel by Amos Tutuola. A grant from the Rockefeller Foundation in 1962 made it possible for Ogunmola to take residence at the University of Ibadan to create a new work and develop a cohesive group of players. With the encouragement of Geoffrey Axeworthy, then director of the school of drama, and Demas Nwoko, a scenic designer and painter, he wrote and composed the music for the folk operatic version of *The Palmwine Drinkard.*

The play opens in Lanke's compound where the Drinkard is reveling in an orgy of palmwine; Ogunmola performed the leading role. Wine gourds drained, the tapster is summoned to provide more. He slips from the top of a palm and falls, breaking his neck. At this point the stage production parts company with the novel. In the book Lanke says upon the death of his tapster, "When I saw that there was no palmwine for me again, one fine morning I took all my native juju (magic charm) and also my father's juju with me . . . and find out whereabout was my tapster who had died."

In the play the hero instead falls into a trance and his subconscious becomes in turn the jungle, the horror-peddling market and Deadstown, the village of the damned.

Describing his design for the Land of the Dead, Demas Nwoko said, "It was a strange country. Nobody's been there and back, so I was free to create any form I liked. The first god was the Night Spirit to which I had to give a body. I thought, Night Spirit, sound of the night—it's musical—night spirits are the owls. I incorporated music of night masquerades and gave them the appearance of night birds, owls, tight-skinned and colorful. The next spirits I gave form to as a white couple because they are laughing at Lanke, who is saying he can do many things. I've put this couple in modern clothes, the man in a proper suit, the woman in a mini, in stockings and high heels and long raffia hair, speaking English in a woodpecker's accent."

The lavish costuming was highly original; a group of female spirits in bright yellow leopard skin had two six-inch stumps shooting out of their breasts. The inhabitants of Deadstown glowered as jet black tubular figures of varying heights. Only a few cutout trees, easily obliterated by lighting, and a series of chairs and benches served as scenery and props.

Lanke proceeds on a hazardous journey. He meets and captures Death, escapes the clutches of the King of the Wicked and finally arrives at Deadstown where he is given the fabled magic egg that turns liquids into palmwine.

*The Palmwine Drinkard* marked the pinnacle of Ogunmola's career, a light-year distant from the slight, moralistic tales such as *Love of Money*, "an ordinary story of everyday people," which was typical of the Traveling Company's repertoire of stories concerned with the perils and corruptions of urban living.

A representative repertoire included *Ore Ogb Eleta* (A successful couple cannot be three), the classic story of a happy family whose life is disrupted by a man who is

37

supposedly a close friend of both husband and wife. After experiencing his deception, the couple expunges him from their lives and is happy again.

In the last few years of Ogunmola's life his productions reflected changing audience attitudes in much the same way as Ogunde's plays. Popular songs were added, with the audience joining the actors in the singing. Also, as did Ogunde, Ogunmola would marry his best actresses in order to keep them in the company. Ogunmola justified polygamy with a matter-of-fact realism:

"I have four wives. If one is running a traveling theater in this country, no matter how poor you may be you are forced to become a polygamist. If you employ an actress today you train her to your taste. When the time comes you want to benefit from the training you have given her; it is then she will tell you she is going to marry. Then you have to start training another. Train them, and make them family, then they are wife as well as worker. Formerly people have been a bit against us but now I must confess that others have been joining us, especially the proprietors of schools. Now they marry more than one wife and train them as school mistresses. That's part of the success of this work in this country."

Two months before Kola Ogunmola died, his Traveling Theatre toured Nigeria's Northern State through all Hausaland. In Kaduna the company performed for over six thousand people at Ahmadu Bello Stadium. Enthusiastic reception of the Hausa-speaking audience to the performance in the Yoruba vernacular established the style of future performances.

Textually more ambitious and musically more interesting than those of Ogunde or Ogunmola, the plays performed by the Duro Ladipo National Theatre range from myth-based tales such as *Oba Koso*, *Oluweri* and *Moremi* to an

African version of *As You Like It* and *Ewe Ayo* (A leaf that is shining for nothing), which is a reworking of the fable of *The Emperor's New Clothes.*

Ladipo's range is enormous. Originally a composer of church music, he fled from the displeasure of the church that banned his music of drums, gongs and shaker instruments as pagan. He then transferred the music of the drums to plays based on Yoruba mythology. A spectacular fusion of movement, music and brilliant costuming, folk operatic theater employs a drum orchestra, flutes and bells to accompany the action and the talking drum, which had been exorcised from the church as being satanic.

As poet and musician, Ladipo has drawn freely on Samuel Johnson's *History of the Yorubas* for source material. Unlike the theater of Ogunde and Ogunmola, Ladipo used written texts. His trilogy of historical tragedies, *Oba Koso, Oba Moro* and *Oba Waja* are actually texts for singing. And, by Ladipo's own admission, nothing pleases him more than to have the audience respond by singing along with the actors.

*Oba Koso* (The king does not hang) is a dramatization of the death and deification as god of thunder of Sango, Alafin (King) of the Oyo Empire in the fourteenth century. Sango is still the central figure of a persistently popular cult and the play, while more theater than ritual drama, is part of a religious experience for Sango worshippers. Certain rituals must precede any performance of *Oba Koso*, Ladipo said. "I cannot perform my plays without rites. For *Oba Koso* the blood of a living animal, like a chicken, must be sucked . . . because the splendor of the majestic gown of Sango is bloody . . . all tied to the ancient past."

The ceremonial dances, too, must reflect tradition accurately, Ladipo said. "You cannot just change the Sango dance for inclusion in *Oba Koso* but you can modify it. You can make it more elaborate. After all, I want people to move. If a mosquito bites you while you are watching my performance, I don't want you to feel it!"

In the tradition of folk operatic companies, Ladipo is artistic creator, writer, composer, choreographer, leading actor and business manager. His plays are not usually reflective of the current political scene, which is of great concern to the playwrights writing in English, such as Soyinka, Rotimi, Aidoo and Nkosi. Ladipo's texts deal mainly with Yoruba legend and history, extended by improvisation. Song, dance, mime and music are all woven into an absorbing spectacle, often overwhelming to a European observer accustomed to non-African theater, which is separated into performance of drama, or of singing, or of dance, seldom an ecstatic coalition of all three.

The verse of a Ladipo text is rich in proverb and imagery. For example, in *Oba Koso*, Gbonka, one of Sango's generals, says,

> "When the elephant dies, we say he falls.
> The Oloromogo tree bleeds without a wound.
> These are the names we give to the king.
> He chases his child through the forest with thunder.
> Thunder is his name!
> But the oracle priest knows secret meanings,
> He alone knows the cause of the elephant's death,
> When the elephant falls—then proverb will clash with
>     proverb!
> But the oracle will reveal
> That I am not their enemy
> And I shall go in peace."

One of Ladipo's most vividly dramatic plays is *Oluweri*, a brief (forty minutes) opera adapted from *Woyengi* by

Obotunde Ijimere, which, in turn, was taken from an Ijaw myth recorded by Gabriel Okara (*Black Orpheus*, No. 2). The theme of the play is based on the concept that man chooses his fate before he is born. Orisawemi, who had been given the magical powers she had requested, is now dissatisfied and wishes to have children instead, a futile expectation since her childless life was her original choice before birth. Determined to have her fate changed, she makes her way back to Oluweri, the creator goddess. Oluweri is furious at Orisawemi's presumption and strips her of all her great magic, intending to kill her. Orisawemi escapes by hiding in the eyes of a pregnant woman. Since that day, the legend and Ladipo's text says that when you look into a person's eyes there is someone looking back at you from inside; it is Orisawemi, the woman who tried to change her fate.

Ulli Beier did much to encourage and guide Ladipo's efforts to create his own company, and a body of folk opera in his unique style. The fruits of their relationship have given immeasurable richness and world-wide recognition to the contemporary folk opera idiom. *Oba Koso* was performed at the Berlin Theatre Festival in 1964, winning first prize, then at the Commonwealth Festival in London, and in Vienna, Holland, Belgium and Frankfurt in 1965. It remains Ladipo's best-known play, and notice of performance has only to be posted to insure standing room only that evening.

Although the dramatists of the folk opera troupes drew generously from the wealth of traditional material, folklore and history, their theater is considered a modern art form. Wole Soyinka, generally accepted as the most important of the African playwrights, noted at the Dakar Negro Arts Festival in 1966 that ". . . folk theater belongs to what we

call the modern Negro-African theater. . . . Because no
art form can be a mere token of traditions . . . [it] demon-
strates by the immediacy of its creativeness the surest touch
on the community's nerve center."

# Concert Party

The transition of drama from festivals, ritual ceremonies and storytelling to the contemporary innovation of concert party is directly related to the influence of the Europeans. New institutions called schools were introduced and a new festival called Empire Day was established by the British colonials. On this day the crowds, dressed in special clothes, all headed for the public park. However, because the Europeans deported themselves differently from Africans, instead of dancing, the schoolchildren marched around in precise formation like battalions of soldiers, returning to stand on platforms and to give what they called a "concert." A concert might include a song in English such as:

> "Brightly, brightly, sun of spring
> Upon this happy day,
> Shine upon us as we sing
> This twenty-fourth of May.
> Shine upon our brothers, too,
> Far across the ocean blue,
> As we raise our songs of praise
> For this our glorious Empire Day."

Holiday crowds flocked to the concerts and were thrilled by the jolly chorales in English. This was a sure sign that the children were progressing for they were singing in the language of the powerful European. Soon the word "concert" became identified with performances given in the European way, on a platform, with the audience seated in front.

Concert parties began among the Fantis of Ghana where the Empire Day interludes became exciting events in the lives of the schoolchildren. Cousin to the church-spawned cantatas of Ogunmola, Ogunde and Ladipo, which were based on biblical stories, concert party plays are secular morality plays, drawn from easily recognizable life situations: the problems of urban life, the evils of prostitution and poverty, self-serving bureaucrats and landlords, the inevitable mother-in-law, the good woman versus the bad woman plus weak man in the middle. The plots are simple and the moral straightforward and direct.

During the second decade of this century a Mr. Yalley, headmaster of an elementary school at Sekondi, put on comic, one-man performances, entertaining his audiences by playing the piano and other instruments and acting at intervals. He dressed in wigs and false moustaches with eyes and mouth painted thickly in white. A young schoolboy named Ishmael Johnson was fascinated by Yalley's one-man show. He and some friends began to stage comic plays themselves, and in 1930 Johnson, Charles Benjamin Hutton and J. B. Ansah formed a concert trio which they called "The Two Bobs and the Carolina Girl." The "two Bobs" were Bob Johnson and Bob Ansah; Hutton, their female impersonator, was the Carolina Girl.

The trio established the classic pattern of the concert play troupe, which is organized around a guitarist, who is always called Bob, and always includes a female impersonator. (In those days a girl on the stage would have been branded a girl without morals. Actresses not being available, the companies resorted to a tradition dating back to Elizabethan theater, with male performers expertly portraying women both in movement and in voice.) The group is always called a "Trio," no matter how many members it has.

The plays were always a combination of music, mime and dance, closely related to American and European vaudeville with plenty of jokes and pretty girls. Villains were booed and the good guys cheered on by the audience.

Much in the same manner as Ogunde's theatrical style, concert party actors improvise on a plot idea rather than use a written script, reacting differently to each night's audience. Starting at about eight o'clock in the evening, a concert party opens with about an hour's worth of popular music, always including the latest hit songs. The stage for the concert party is an open platform, surrounded on three sides by seats. At the end of the music portion of the program, the instruments are removed from the platform and the actors make their entrance from the side and back. They poke fun at the greedy landlord, the conniving government official, or the young man still provincial enough to believe in the power of juju over the virtue of hard work. The criticism is usually handled with a light satiric touch but not so subtle as to be missed.

Efua Sutherland, the Ghanaian playwright, described one hilarious routine of a trio concerned with the government's effort to encourage people to return to the farms. "If you're poor," the actor in the play said, "listen to this: the price of land is lower, so is the price of spades and hoes. Hey! Dying's your best bet. Die now, while it's cheap!"

No matter what the plot, the concert party performance

is meant to be funny. Even the most lugubrious story will have fast dances and laughter-provoking costumes; the faces of the performers very often are painted black, with lips, nose and eyebrows painted white. Pillows get stuffed into shirts to make outrageously fat stomachs, wigs of startling structure are worn, as well as very tight, very colorful pants.

The greatest of the Bobs, Bob Johnson, tells how he came to use the name Bob for any comedy actor. Playing around the premises of the Optimism Club close to his home, he and his friends would watch the club members, and sometimes run errands for them.

"Some American Negroes used to come there for drinks," says Johnson, "and they would send us boys on little errands. I was always alert and willing and quick, so I was a favorite errand boy. When those American Negroes called us they said, 'Say, Bob!' So it became a habit among ourselves to call one another 'Bob' just for fun. When we were planning our first shows it was natural for us to call the characters we wanted as jokers, 'Bob'."

In 1960 the Ghana National Entertainment Association listed twenty-eight different guitar bands or concert parties, including Ahanta Trio, Bob Cole's Ghana Trio, Black Star Trio, Fanti Trio, Builder's Brigade Concert Party, the Jaguar Jokers and Onyina's Guitar Band.

The Two Bobs and the Carolina Girl toured the Gold Coast for seven years until Bob Johnson left the group to join a Cape Coast dance band known as The Sugar Babies. Renamed The Axim Trio, it became enormously successful, traveling through West Africa, and becoming so much in demand that hardly any celebration or festival of importance could be planned without including a performance by the group.

Long narrative songs are a specialty of a concert party

known as The African Brothers. Along with the Highlife rhythms of an organ, snare drum, bongo drum, a slit gong, beaded gourd rattle and two guitars (all aided with an amplification system), The African Brothers perform such epic sagas as the narrative song about a man with two wives. To one wife he has given a goat, to the other a deer. Each wife is unhappy with her gift and because they like each other, they conspire to remedy the situation. Deciding to confront him at his office, they descend on their husband at his desk, pouring out their grievances as he desperately tries to continue typing. The audience roars with laughter when at last the boss tries to read his employee's typed report, with its incomprehensible mixture of stock inventory and price schedules and unwanted gifts of goat and deer.

Songs performed at concert parties are often recorded. If they deal with a topical subject, they sell out quickly. One example is "Ebi Te Yie," a play on words, which means literally, "You are well seated" or "You are living well." The song describes a meeting of all the animals to discuss their mutual welfare. The leopard, sitting behind the antelope, bullied and tormented it, pinning down his tail with his claws and shouting the antelope down when he began to speak. The intimidation became so unbearable that the antelope finally shouted out, "Petition, please, on a point of order, chairman. I suggest we adjourn to another day because not all of us are well seated, ebi te yie; others are not well seated at all, ebi nnte yie". The song became a top-selling record and the phrase became part of the shorthand jargon used by Ghanaians.

Never a passive spectator, the African audience at the concert party performance continues to be involved with the action on the stage, doubled over with laughter one minute, weeping in sympathy the next. The audience will often express its feelings with gifts of money—sometimes by marching directly on stage to place the money in the hands or shoe of the performer, or by sticking a coin on the forehead (the ultimate praise) of one of the actors.

Men have been known to rush up to a performing group to perform their own dance, and women will walk right on stage to present a good performer with their own head ties. When a song as popular and as significant as "Ebi Te Yie" is sung, the audience will literally shower the actors with coins.

Performance by the Oak Theatre of the University of Nigeria, Nsukka (at the 1972 Ife Festival of the Arts) of "EDUFA" by Ghanaian playwright Efua Southerland

# University-Based Theater

**W**hile Ladipo and Ogunmola and the guitar bands known as concert parties were bringing their style of theatrical entertainment to remote villages, university-based groups, greatly influenced by Western culture, were deepening the content of drama.

The creation of schools of drama, drama workshops, competitions sponsored for original works, as well as the production of European classics, synthesized the traditional African form of song, dance, story and mime with Western style proscenium theater into a new African theater of vigor, originality and beauty.

Although Africans began to write plays in the 1880's in Lagos, few of them were published. Drama was dependent on the self-sustaining energies of each group and the encouragement of the colonial administration. Small public halls and schoolrooms were requisitioned as theaters.

Missionary activities at the turn of the century accelerated in pace with those of the colonial administration, particularly in the crusade against the festivals denigrated as primitive and superstitious. Most mission schools encouraged plays that were invariably dramatized versions of scripture histories. Their moralistic guidelines for plots are much in evidence in the plays performed by students today.

Easy to act, and requiring only single staging and costuming, the school plays have become integral to standard curriculum.

Among the most famous of this genre is *The Incorruptible Judge* by D. Olu Olagoke. Uncomplicated in construction, the play's main characters are a young man applying for a job, the corrupt employer who habitually demands a dash (bribe) for the privilege of being employed and the stalwart, incorruptible judge in front of whom the bribe-hungry employer finally appears.

The school-type of play, in fact, does not refer only to plays performed at schools but generally to the literature of plays teaching a lesson, such as the inevitability of retribution for greed or for disrespect for tradition. A now classic theme in modern African drama, the impact of urbanization on traditional society is ubiquitous not only in the simple school play but in the work of the major African dramatists.

In somewhat the same way theater was used for educational purposes in a program established in Ghana in 1948 (known then as Gold Coast). Touring teams of players presented short plays, which demonstrated such virtues as self-improvement through education, the value of good hygiene and the importance of paying one's taxes; each play was followed by a discussion. In a typical story, a young man chooses a plain but literate girl as his wife, rather than her beautiful sister, who thereupon enrolls in a literacy class.

And, in the fifties, the Lagos Child Welfare Mother's Union used the simple play as its chief medium for propaganda. The Union was an expression of the right of women to protest when things were going wrong. Masculine folly was the theme of one of their plays, which were usually produced either in a public hall or an open space in the street.

School plays, the church-based dramas and the tradition-inspired folk operas all served to highlight the growing self-awareness of the emerging, independent African countries. In villages and towns audiences gathered to be entertained by these groups of traveling actors and musicians, although they were not yet educated to the Western ways of audience response, such as applauding at specified intervals of acts and final curtain.

African drama, ancient and rich in heritage, was never a static art, separated from function and the spiritual statements of a people. As a living medium of expression it continued to develop as the Western world more and more encroached on the traditional African way of life. With the colonial governments and the missionaries came formal schools, the teaching of English and French, reading and writing and, finally, the universities. It is at the higher institutions of learning that the most significant contributions to drama have been made. The modern African universities, supported by government money, are today the wellspring of dramatic African literature. The plays of Soyinka, Aidoo, Clark, Rotimi and Sutherland—all of whom in some measure deal with the dramatic conflict of the collision of old ways and new life-styles—represent much of contemporary drama production at university theater departments in Ghana and Nigeria.

Dance and music, traditionally combined with the proverbs and allegory of the storyteller's presentation, are now fashioned into modern dramas designed for modern stages. Often traditional forms of music and dance are used to express modern concerns. *Kongi's Harvest* by Wole

Soyinka, for example, is a tragedy about a dictator who opposes the forces of tradition and is finally deserted by all but a bodyguard or two. The play had a world premiere at Dakar in the ultramodern Daniel Sorano Theatre. It is a political satire on the dictatorial tendencies that have manifested themselves in the developing African states. The resemblance of Kongi to Kwame Nkrumah, ex-president of Ghana, is an obvious one, although program note disclaimers are made as, for example, at the performance of *Kongi's Harvest* at the Ife Festival of the Arts when it was asserted that the play was "not about Kongi but Kongism, not about ex-president Nkrumah but the practice of Kongism which has never been dethroned in Black Africa."

Tradition tears through the outer layer of modern reference at the grand climax of the Yam Festival in *Kongi's Harvest* with its boisterous chanting, dancing and parading and the booming sound of a hundred pounding pestles. The unbroken links to the past are everywhere in Soyinka's plays. *A Dance of the Forest*, presented as part of the celebration for Nigeria's independence, deals with a people's relationship to its past. At a ceremony symbolic of Nigeria's independence, resurrected ancestors are rejected by the living who, disillusioned with a past they thought would give them strength for the future, want only the present, although they find the past impossible to deny.

Ritual, dance and a ceremonial masking at the play's end again identify Soyinka's work as a blend of Western and African style. The play, *A Dance of the Forest*, as a whole is a dance, divided into three parts or movements, rather than acts. As Soyinka put it, ". . . our forms of theater are quite different from literary drama. We use spontaneous dialogue, folk music, simple stories and relevant dances to express what we mean. Our theater uses stylized forms as its basic disciplines. I am trying to integrate these forms into the drama of the English language."

The comic play, *The Lion and the Jewel*, is one of the most popular of all Soyinka's works. Written in verse form, the story of the seduction of beautiful and arrogant Sidi by the wily old Bale of the village is again a reflection of the Africa of tradition and today. Sidi's modern young suitor, Lakunle, stubbornly refuses to pay the traditional bride price in order to marry her. She will not sacrifice her dignity by marrying without it. The Bale, head man of the village, symbol of tradition, with a leonine potency un-dimmed by years, captures the jewel, Sidi, for his own. In the last scene of the play she shoves Lakunle away from her, saying,

> "Out of my way, book-nourished shrimp.
> Do you see what strength he has given me?
> That was not bad for a man of sixty.
> It was the secret of God's own draught,
> A deed for drums and ballads."

Imagery and poetic idiom are found throughout African dramatic literature in various styles. *The Gods Are Not to Blame*, Ola Rotimi's prize-winning treatment of the Oedipus theme, is rich in imagery and proverb: "But joy has a slender body that breaks too soon." "When rain falls on the leopard, does it wash off its spots? Has the richness of kingly life washed off the love of our King for his people?" In *Kurunmi*, Rotimi's play about the nineteenth century Yoruba war between Ijaye and Ibadan, Kurunmi's tragedy is expressed in the lines he speaks when all is lost to him: "It is not the beating of raindrops that hurts, it is the touch of dew, the soft touch of dew."

Side by side with traditional drama a modern African theater is being formed, which exploits the ideas and techniques of the European stage. The use of verse and ritual structure distinguishes John Pepper Clark's *Song of a Goat*, for example, as a classic treatment of a classic theme, the inevitability of a curse that sets the tragedy in motion. The problem of Zifa's impotence in *Song of a Goat*, which might have been given a psychological interpretation in a European drama, is, in Clark's play, the result of a curse.

A more contemporary treatment of tragedy is worked into the character of Edufa, the Faustian figure in the play of that name by Efua Sutherland. Although *Edufa* is built on a foundation of traditional African ritual sacrifice, the spiritual conflict is explored in the context of a modern, fashionable, rich man's home. While the husband discovers the futility of trying to escape the consequences of his pact to preserve his life and fortune at the cost of his wife's life, there is unmistakable reference to Edufa's own responsibility for the tragic rewards of his greed and self-importance.

*The Masquerade*, Clark's second play, not only shares character links with *Song of a Goat* but is also based solely and literally on a tragic theme rooted in legend. The characters speak Clark's rich and vivid verse but never emerge as real people in lifelike situations. It is in his play, *The Raft*, that Clark fuses traditional roots and modern day Africa. The play is about four lumbermen taking a raft down the Niger. They drift helplessly, and their predicament is meant to indicate the tragedy of people unable to work together and, more specifically, suggests Nigeria's torment as she searches for direction while floating in the hazardous waters of the modern Western world. The men are Africans, secure in their traditional beliefs with little regard for the ways of the white man. Finally they are all destroyed, either in body or in spirit.

One of the most interesting of the current plays using this same theme of conflict is *The Dilemma of a Ghost* by Ama Ata Aidoo, now a lecturer at the University of Cape Coast. In the play, an American Negro woman journeys with her African-born husband to his home and family, and into a situation typical of fractious in-law relationships. The quarrels, however, are based on the larger theme of the chasm between the black worlds of Africa and the United States of America, and the realization that notwithstanding a similarity in skin color, the product of American society is alien to the African's life-style, ignorant of and unable to deal successfully with his traditions.

Another example of Western and African influence took place on the first of December, 1972, at the Centre for Nigerian Culture Studies of Ahmadu Bello University in Kano. A dramatized version of the late Alhaji Sir Abubakar Tafawa Balewa's novel, *Shaihu Umar*, was presented at a command performance for General Gowon, the head of the Nigerian government. Both Western and African influences are found in *Shaihu Umar*. For instance, the Calypso singer is a familiar character in Trinidad, with his highly gifted political and social sense, a self-imposed obligation to right wrongs, using the powerful weapon of ridicule and the opportunity to sing praise songs for money. A Hausa version of the Calypsonian was introduced into the cast as a sort of town crier, as a messenger from the warrior who has been deported, and as a praise singer.

Although *Shaihu Umar* was presented in the Hausa language, the range of cultural contexts was wide, since locales in the play included both pagan and Islamic Hausaland, the Sahara, North Africa and Egypt. Another innovation was the use of the goge and kukuma instruments. Both are one-stringed instruments, the kukuma being high-pitched, the goge low-pitched. Each was used to represent a character on stage, their rhythms and melody lines paralleling the actions of the representative actors.

The play itself is a gorgeous modern version of the old storyteller's art. In the famous dream sequence the storyteller, Shaihu Umar, is in Kagara, Nigeria, as he narrates the recurring dream he had as a young man in Ber Kufa, Egypt. When a boy he had been kidnapped in Hausaland and was added as a special gift to a slave shipment going to Ber Kufa. His owner befriended him and educated him as his own son. Shaihu Umar's dream was about a lioness losing her cub to hunters and her efforts to find him in the desert.

The action of the dream is on stage right and, interspersed throughout the dream narrative, the real search by his own mother is seen during the play on the left half of the stage. An Arab of Tripoli, Ahmad, represents the "reality" acting area. The events of dream and reality, of course, parallel each other and culminate in the capture of the lioness and Shaihu Umar's tragic reunion with his mother, as she dies in his arms.

This production was considered a turning point in the local effort to research Hausa cultural material in its detailed and scholarly study of Hausa dress, decorative ideas and musical forms. On a broader scale, however, it was merely one more instance of the vital role the university plays in identifying with the cultural reawakening of the African people.

Performance by the University of Ife Theatre Company of Muraina Oyelami's "Alo Ipada" (based on a Papuan variation of the Orpheus-in-the-underworld theme)

# The Audience:
## *Language and Laughter*

The African writer represents a culture in which the arts are an integral part of the life-style. Anyone with even a superficial acquaintance with the African way of life is aware that Africans have always placed great importance on the functional worth of an art form. The African writer, responsive to the ever-increasing span of Western influence, must make his own decision as to the audience he wishes to reach, the "educated" African who understands English or those who understand only the vernacular tongue.

Education in English is a prestigious accomplishment, but African English is far from the King's English and equally removed from the American's style of speech. Writer Dennis Duerden notes that "African writers and university scholars to whom I have been talking have been sealed off from the modern urban population as well. They have been selected to spend their school lives in boarding schools and from there go to universities at home or abroad. The English they speak and write compared with the English spoken in the towns of Africa can be compared to medieval Latin in relation to medieval English, despite the fact that it is our own English."

Efua Sutherland, in an interview with Maxine Lautre in *African Writers Talking* discusses the difficulty African audiences experience when viewing plays in English: "I maintain that it is in theater that we are discovering what a foreign language English is, because our productions in English have a long way to go to achieve standards, because we don't wear the language comfortably. . . . I think there will come a time when English becomes a Ghanaian language, not a foreign one."

Agreement varies among writers on this issue. Ola Rotimi declared that since he was educated in English (and is a product of the Yale Drama School) he feels most comfortable in English.

Both Duro Ladipo and Kola Ogunmola produced their body of folk opera in the vernacular. For Dexter Lyndersay the solution was to accommodate both, by providing program notes in English to plays in vernacular, as he did, for example, in his production of *Shaihu Umar*, performed in Hausa. At the Arts Theatre, University of Ibadan, the School of Drama Acting Company presented *A 'Are Akogun*, a Nigerian tragedy of the supernatural (based on Shakespeare's *Macbeth*), in both Yoruba and English dialogue. The play was directed by Wale Ogunyemi and Dexter Lyndersay. As the play opens the drums say,

"Erù Oba ni mo bà
  Oba to!
  I dread the king,
  The all powerful."

And the men sing,

"Érée yin la wá se
Tèlà omo ki la ri fOba se
Iràan yin la wá wò o,
Tèlà omo ki la ri fOba se.
It is you we come to entertain
Tela, what harm can one do to a king.
It is your performance we've come to see
Tela, what harm can one do to a king."

Such recourse to the use of both vernacular and English was also demonstrated in George Wilson's production of the folk opera by Saka Acquaye, *The Lost Fisherman*, presented at the Arts Council Theatre in Accra, in which the spoken dialogue was in English but the songs were performed in Ga.

More and more the spoken word of the African stage reflects the familiar position of the African writer straddling two worlds. Often a playwright will shuttle back and forth from English to pidgin. In Soyinka's *Trials of Brother Jero*, for example, Chume, provoked into hysteria, alters his correct English to "Help 'am quick quick!" And, in *The Road*, Soyinka has Samson, a lorry driver, imitating the character of the Professor whom he believes is distributing bribes, "Ah, my friends, what can I do for you?" then reverting to his comfortable self, saying, "God I go chop lifemake I tell true. I go chop the life to tey God go jealous me. And if he take jealousy kill me I will go start bus service between heaven and hell."

"Pidgin," according to Demas Nwoko, the set designer of *The Palmwine Drinkard*, "is the type of English in which you can express your vernacular self. "I easily jump into pidgin; it is not a language of class. The words are introduced as the need arises. One can say 'depth' is good English if you wanted to say, 'from the depth of my heart.' Well, the heart has no depth; the *belly* has depth. You feed it, it must be a pit, it has *depth.* It is easier to say 'from the bottom of my belly' but that's vulgar, that's bad English, so in pidgin you say, 'bottom belly.' In a play about ideas, you have to write as the people speak."

Even the storyteller, the stalwart repository of tradition, is touched by this phenomenon of duality of language. With travel to different villages no longer an occasional event, the curiosity of each tribe about others is sharpened with a resultant interchange of ideas and a need to express respective customs to others. If the village storyteller is unable to communicate with those who speak different languages, then he must give way to the younger and usually Western educated storyteller who can offer his stories not only in the vernacular but in English as well.

Although Africans long ago accepted the reality of the colonial conquerors, their anger at the effrontery of one group of people imposing their religion, culture and moral code on another is still alive and articulated. Duro Ladipo's contempt for the white bishop who banned his drums from the church service as being "dirty" echoes the feelings of a great many Africans.

Segun Olusola, one of Nigeria's foremost talents in the theater and television said, "I feel *deprived* that I cannot express all of the things I want to say at all times in Yoruba. This is a fault of my upbringing, my associations in my later life. English is a convenient language which we cannot do without. But there is always for me this underlying depression, this underlying feeling of deprivation that we have to hang on [to English] for most of the deeper things we are doing, those of us who are writing or communicating in any form. For me, the desire would be to communicate first in that language [vernacular of the region]. Naturally, if we're beginning to think of a television public, then we will look at the market we are serving and then decide whether that market appreciates programs in the English language more than in any other."

But dramatic communication can be achieved in more than one way and when spoken dialogue is not understood, then body movement, mime and dance and gestures can serve as artistic expression. Dance is a direct form of dramatic and theatrical communication. Even without speech, expressive body movements involve even the most unsophisticated member of the audience in the theme of the story. The introduction of disciplined dance movements into theatrical production is new and fascinating and dance dramas such as *Alatangana*, for example, are enormously appealing. Based on a creation myth of the Kono of Guinea, its musical and dance themes have been drawn from various Nigerian cultures. Dance movements from the Ijaw, Kaniberi, Yoruba, Lopawa, Ibo, Itsekiri and Ika cultures have been used as a basis for dramatic expression in theatrical productions. Reviewing a performance of *Alatangana* at the World Festival of Theatre at Nancy, France, the critic Yolande Thiviet in *Le Journal de Nancy* said of the production, "Everything, the percussion, the masks and the costumes, participate in this search for modernization which leads traditional Africa into the present without losing her vitality and her own originality."

Expressive body movement is typical of the African acting style in dialogue plays as well as in dance dramas. Gestures are broad and exaggerated. A woman weeping, for example, is likely to strike her head with her hand, almost in biblical style of breast-beating as a gesture of woe. Clenching a fist under the chin and striking one's head is a sign of remorse. Wiggling a thumb in the direction of another person means that the one to whom it is pointed is a fool.

These physically defined phrases are immediately understood without dialogue. A young Yoruba boy, for instance, talking to an elder, wouldn't stand with his arms behind his back for that would be a sign of impudence. He must prostrate himself. Or, during a quarrel between two chiefs, when a messenger is sent to the rival, he sticks a leaf between his lips. This signifies that the messenger is not responsible for whatever message he is obliged to deliver and requests protection until he is back in his own village.

Whatever effect the colonialists, the missionaries and the ever-increasing flow of Western-style clothes, furniture and electronic marvels have had on the African's life-style, he remains steadfastly African, reacting fully, participating totally as a member of an audience for music, theater or music-hall vaudeville.

The audience, as much a part of the performance as the actors, provides endings to proverbs, takes up the chorus of chants, comments on the dialogue, punctuates stories with exclamations or disapproval. When Moremi sings her broken-hearted farewell to her son in Ladipo's folk opera of that name, the audience more than likely will join in with her, sharing her sadness and her song.

Audience participation, African style, is not dissimilar to the American tradition of hissing the villain and cheering the hero. What causes profound amazement, however, is the African's response of giggles, guffaws and uproarious laughter to the most dramatic and awful moments of staged tragedy. A now legendary anecdote about this phenomenon concerns the 1964 tour of the Nottingham Players who brought *Macbeth* to Nigeria. In the sleep-walking scene the audiences roared their heads off and the English company was literally dumbfounded.

This reaction is not reserved for the work of European dramatists. At performances of *Edufa* by Efua Sutherland, for example, an African play with African actors, the audience usually finds the scene where the wife is dying an irresistible provocation for hysterical laughter. This unexpected reponse is a source of embarrassment and confusion to African sociologists and theater people alike. Explanations are varied; perhaps Africans laugh at tragedy on stage because they know the actors are only acting and they are not really dead, or possibly their laughter is a cathartic reaction, a release of tension.

Another theory is that African audiences are only skeptical; when a man pays a fee to enter a theater, to sit down and watch a play, he's still connected to the world of realism. While the acting company is doing its best to convince him of the seriousness of the action, he's laughing and saying to himself, "I'm not convinced yet."

Unlike Western audiences who groan inwardly at poor histrionics, trying to accept a moment as tragic because the actors act as if it were, the African audience does not feel it necessary to pretend what it doesn't feel. As Dexter Lyndersay put it, "I will back a Nigerian audience against Sir Laurence Olivier anytime. If he says that is a tragic moment and my Nigerian audience laughs, I say, 'It wasn't well done, sorry.' "

At the end of a performance an African audience is likely merely to rise and leave. Their involvement with the play, continuous and rapt during performance, is finished at the play's end; applause is a Western custom. In no way is the African audience obediently responsive to a preordained code of response. When one is part of an African audience, he is constantly aware of its aliveness, its vitality and a totally and uninhibited honesty of reaction. Perhaps after another century of Westernization, the African will learn to applaud at the right time. It is a transformation many observers hope never takes place.

Performance of the Actor's Studio in Accra, Ghana, of "Song of a Goat" by Nigerian playwright John Pepper Clark

# Drama on the Move

Ananse, the spider, West Africa's folk hero, has traveled all the way from the storyteller's moonlit compound to the klieg-lit sound stage of the Ghana Film Industry Corporation. His odyssey depicts the increasing Western worldliness of African theater arts and the wide use of folk material. From the fireside where the old man sang and danced and mimicked has come many of the stories of the trickster spider man, the cycle of tales known as Anansesem, the stories of Ananse. This disreputable knave not only caught the fancy of the old tellers of tales but of contemporary playwrights and film makers. He is as enduring as traditional Africa herself, surfacing, in fact, across the Atlantic as B'rer Rabbit. (Both spider and rabbit are protagonists in stories of cunning crime and shameful punishments.)

Ananse emerges as the main character in *Ananse and the Gum Man*, an original play by Joe de Graft, presented at the Ghana Drama Studio with a full cast of characters. The play was so successful that the Ghana Film Industry Corporation used it for its first feature-length film, adapted by Ato Kwamina Yanney, produced and directed by Sam

Aryeetey, with David Longdon, a multi-talented Ghanaian actor as Ananse. It has been shown continuously since 1965, reputedly never to less than a full house, and in 1969 won second prize at the Film Festival in Melbourne, Australia. A good part of the dialogue is in the language of Twi and is partially ad-libbed.

A dearth of supportive funds has hampered creative talents in the most modern medium of communication today, television. Africa, called a cinematographical desert in the early 1960's, has not yet become an oasis of film or television. Television is still a luxury throughout the continent, with not even one percent of black Africa having access to the medium. The high cost of broadcasting facilities, the lack of electrification and trained personnel all make up a formidable combination of difficulties. Heavy reliance on canned programming from America is still evident in the television logs; "I Love Lucy," "Perry Mason," "Bonanza," et cetera, appear daily. An estimated seventy-five percent of television programming is foreign.

The first television program in black Africa was broadcast from an old Parliament building in Ibadan, Western Nigeria, in 1959. Whereas film preceded television in most African countries, only a few, notably the French-speaking nations, really developed the medium to any extent. In a UNESCO report to the United Nations, the situation was summed up as follows: "Most of the countries of tropical Africa lack film production facilities of any kind. Existing production units are hampered by a dearth of development capital and trained personnel, the high cost of importing raw film and equipment generally subject to import duties and difficulties in organizing adequate distributive systems."

Unlike the countries of the Western world where television talent naturally derived from the vast experience of years of professional theater and film, African television had no such heritage.

The first full-length play in English especially produced for television was broadcast in 1961 over WNTV (Nigeria). Written by Wole Soyinka and directed by Segun Olusola, *My Father's Burden* featured many of the leading talents from the amateur stage. Ghanaian television aired an adaptation of Molière's *Tartuffe*, which was called *Osofo Moko*. In 1966 a program called "On Stage" was introduced, a half-hour show of improvised drama and free expression. In addition to the established companies of Ladipo and Ogunmola performing their traditional plays for "On Stage," the comic theater of Moses Olaiya, alias Baba Sala, was a great favorite of television audiences.

Major original television productions have been based on such popular plays as Clark's *Song of a Goat*, *Dilemma of a Ghost* by Ama Ata Aidoo and *The New Patriots* by Sarif Easmon, a work concerned with political corruption. In 1968, the inevitable television serial was developed, a half-hour weekly based on a story entitled "The Village Headmaster." The title character is a recurring figure in village life, the all-wise father figure to whom people came for advice and judgment.

In the following excerpt from the original master script of *The Village Headmaster*, initially conceived as a feature film, both vernacular and pidgin English are used. Adapting it for television, its creator, Segun Olusola, recognized that about eighty percent of the viewing population understand and speak Yoruba.

Africa is beset with more than the typical problems faced by the creative arts. While insufficient money is the prime concern, particularly difficult climatic conditions also present obstacles. Since ceremonial events are so important in the lives of most Africans, what is needed—in addition to air-conditioned television studios—is equipment that can bring these events from the market square to the home. Furthermore, the virtual absence of full-time professional actors and actresses and of professional theaters makes it necessary for the television industry to be heavily dependent on amateur groups. There is already proof of talent in the written material for the medium.

Television was preceded by filmmaking in most African countries, yet only a few, notably the Francophone (French-speaking) developed the medium to any extent. As is the case in television production there is widespread lack of film production facilities, an impediment that is compounded by a dearth of developing capital and trained personnel, the high cost of importing raw film and equipment and the difficulty in organizing adequate distribution centers.

Although film production varies from country to country and is directly related to indigenous politics and economics, concern about foreign control of film distribution is expressed by filmmakers across the continent. There are large numbers of European and American owned and financed movie houses all over Africa. If African filmmakers were able to control distribution, production schedules could be projected on the basis of known and anticipated profits. The conditions of film production are linked to conditions of film distribution which, in most African countries, have not changed significantly since pre-independence days and are seriously blocking the development of the industry.

The individual movie maker is forced to exert as much creative initiative in locating working capital as in making the film itself. Ousmane Sembene, black Africa's most famous cinema director, in an interview at the University of Wisconsin, said, "Sometimes you can find a friend with credit at the bank who will let you use that credit." Not surprisingly, African filmmakers have to depend heavily on foreign funds as well as technical skill in the production of major films. Again, as in television and the stage, there is a virtual absence of full-time professional actors, making the film industry dependent on amateurs with all of the attendant problems of insufficient rehearsals, lack of discipline and the resultant sub-standard performances.

But soaring beyond all handicaps is Africa's imperative to correct the false images imposed by European and American filmmakers in movies about Africa where the continent was only decor and the African only actor, and the need to accurately describe African history showing the European as the ruthless and relentless invader. "Filmmaking in a developing country," said Sam Aryeetey of the Ghana Film Corporation, "should be seen as part of nation building, dramatizing local problems and achievements in terms of local idiom and experience, the interpretation of ourselves *to* ourselves and to other people."

Movies such as "Sanders of the River" and "The Heart of the Matter" which glorified colonialism are now as inappropriate as the absurd Tarzan saga. African filmmakers are almost totally concerned with changing the image of themselves as seen through the colonialists' lens and Sembene is only one of many African directors who are committed to the ideal of using film to rebuild a sense of cultural identity and tradition disrupted by colonialism. His film, "Le Mandat" (The Money Order), is considered an archetype of the new cinema, not only in his native Senegal but of Africa in general. "Le Mandat" (in its Wolofized version shown as "Mandabi") depicts the plight of an uneducated African who tries to cash a gift money order from his nephew in France. He is humiliated and finally cheated out of both his money and his home by the neo-colonial bureaucracy and all those who parasitically exploit it.

Corruption as the legacy of Western-imposed morality is used again and again by Sembene. "Borom Sarret" is a powerful piece of film about a day in the life of a carter and a bitter restatement of the terrible truth of individual suffering so unbearable that each one is unable to pity the fate of others. "La Noire de . . ." (The Black Girl"), awarded first prize for the best full length film at the Festival of Negro Arts at Dakar in 1966, reflects Sembene's conviction that in spite of poverty and misery, the dignity of the poor is immutable and more constant than that of the rich, and that what saved Africa from total destruction during colonial assault was its stubborn hold on its own image of respectability.

Sembene, in concert with other Senegalese filmmakers (Ababacar Samb, Paulin Vieyra, Blaise Senghor) has produced film dramaturgy that makes up in commitment to the ideal of an indigenous art form what it lacks in technical finesse and acting skill. He is primarily responsible for Dakar's position as film center of black Africa. The collision between the irresistible force of modernity and the immovable fact of tradition is the dramatic focus for most of the films. "Kodou", made by Ababacar Samb in 1971, describes the anguish of a young girl who defies the ancient ritual of lip tatooing and then suffers the consequences of derision by the villagers, and the guilt of bringing shame and dishonor to her parents. Samb's prize-winning "Et La Neige N'Etait Plus" (And the Snow Was No More) turns on a now-classic theme of contemporary African drama, about the university graduate who, returned from Europe to his village home, finds himself confronted with ancestral tradition with which he has lost touch. It is the reverse treatment of another primary concern of most films, the odyssey from village to urban life.

The majority of film production is currently centered in West Africa and include such examples as, from Nigeria: Francis Oladele's "Kongi's Harvest" and "Things Fall Apart"; Ivory Coast: "Sur La Dune de la Solitude" by Timite Bassori; Niger: Mustapha Alassane's animated experiments, "Le Voyage de Sim" and "La Mart de Gandji"; Dahomey: "Sous Le Signe du Vondou" made by Pascal Abikanlou; Mauritania: Med Hondo's production, "Les Bicots" and again from Senegal, the splendid documentaries by Paulin Vieyra such as "Lamb" about wrestling, Senegal's national sport and Tidiane Aw's "Réalitié" in which a ritual ceremony to cure mental illness is reenacted for the camera.

In the Republic of Chad, Edouard Sailly has devoted himself to making newsreels about the country. But his masterpiece is the first African film to use only sound, with no dialogue or added commentary to explain images. "Le Troisieme Jour" (The Third Day) was made in 1966. It tells the story of a young man who, suffering the loss of a dear one, uses the three day period of time it takes for a soul to reach heaven to explore his own sense of being in a silent devotion. This silence, more revealing than long discourse, marks the effective density of the drama.

In East Africa, documentaries comprise Uganda's main output while Tanzania's first feature film saw completion as recently as 1974, "Fimbo ya Mnyonge." South Africa, where the struggle against apartheid persists against awesome odds is the venue for one of Africa's most significant films, "Last Grave at Dimbaza." It was secretly shot in 1973 at one of South Africa's notorious resettlement camps and smuggled to Britain where it was shown at the National Film Theatre. Eventually it won the Committed Film Award at Grenoble. "Last Grave at Dimbaza" is powerful propaganda filled with terrible ironies such as the sequence where a black nanny, whose son has died of malnutrition, carefully feeds her white charge.

There is an old African saying regarding the difference between a wise and a foolish man: A foolish man is like the river which comes to a boulder in the middle and tries to move it. It is the wise river that goes around it, leaves it and moves steadily forward. The new playwrights, the creative talents in film and television, though employing Western techniques, relate steadfastly to traditions of the past. African culture, the same as culture in any other part of the world, is merely human experience as it meets difficulties and conquers them. According to Wole Soyinka, the artist functions in African society ". . . as the voice of vision in his own time." One could say of African theater in general what is said of African cultures in general—that it goes on developing at its own rate, absorbing into itself those foreign influences encountered by it, emerging uniquely as itself.

Scenes from Nigerian Duro Ladipo's "Oba Kosa"
(The King Did Not Hang) performed in Lagos by
the Duro Ladipo Nation Theatre Company

Performance by the University of Ife Theatre Company of Muraina Oyelami's "Alo Ipada" (based on a Papuan variation of the Orpheus-in-the-underworld theme)

Performance by the University of Ife Theatre Company (at the 1972 Ife Festival of the Arts) of Leopold Senghor's (President of Senegal) "Chaika"

# The Palmwine Drinkard
## KOLA OGUNMOLA (Excerpt)
### *Scene:* Encounter With A God

*A man with a white beard who wears European clothes sits with his wife. He is enjoying himself with wine in a place decorated with a radio, a refrigerator, an electric fan and other things. Lànké comes in and greets them. Man and wife speaking in spirit language.*

LÀŃKÉ: Greetings, father!
    Greetings, Madam!
    Greetings on this time of the day!
    I hope you are having a good rest!
    Greetings on your relaxation!

MAN AND WIFE: You are welcome!
    Greetings on your journey!
    Please, where are you from?
    How did you come here?
    Where are you going?

LÀŃKÉ: Even if you don't know an elephant, have you never heard the trumpeting of an elephant?
    Even if you don't know the lagoon, have you never added salt to soup?
    Even if you don't know me, haven't you heard my voice, Lànké's?
    I am Lànké the Drinker!
    I am the one who cleans his mouth with palmwine on awakening!

I was born in the midst of wealth!
I was brought up in the midst of riches!
Are you listening to me?
I have a calabash for palmwine at home.
And I have many palm trees in the farm.
Palmwine gourds are numberless in my room!
My tapper it was who fell down!
As he was tapping palmwine he fell
And death came!
For me, Lànké, and all my friends.
"The squirrel had climbed the ìrókò tree, leaving the
    hunter staring."
Then there was no palmwine for us to drink
And so we became enemies of one another!
I thought and thought,
I decided and made up my mind
To go to the town of the dead
And bring back my palmwine tapper!
This is why you see me here, my father!
There is no wine as delicious
As that of my Àlàbá!

MAN: You want to take back someone who has died?

LÀŃKÉ: It is so!

WIFE: And you believe that it will be possible?

LÀŃKÉ: It must be possible!
    I am Father-of-the-gods,
    I can do anything in the world!
    Just show me the way to the town of the dead.
    Please,

I will go and return!
When the hand goes to the mouth, it must return!

MAN AND WIFE: If it is so,
Before we show you the way,
We must test you
And you must pass the test!

MAN: Go to the house of the blacksmith:
The blacksmith I asked to do some work for me.
Go and bring the thing I asked him to make.
The thing has no name!
If you can find the house of the blacksmith
And bring back the thing,
I will agree that you are Father-of-the gods!
We shall make a way for you to take
To find your palmwine tapper!

[*Laughter. Drumming. Husband and wife look at Lànké critically. They look at each other. Lànké goes out.*]

WIFE: My husband, listen now!
I want to ask a question.
What is the matter with human beings?
What are they running after in the world?
If you see them any time,
They are always in difficulty!
I don't understand it!
Maybe you can explain it to me!

MAN: Ah! Thank you, thank you, thank you.
The question you asked is a good one!
It is sensible!

How to get food and drink and how to become rich
Are the preoccupations of human beings!
None of them ever has enough!
They are never satisfied!
All this is responsible for the troubles
Of human beings!
This is an example!
He wants to go to the town of the dead!
He wants to bring home his palmwine tapper who is
    dead!

[*They laugh.*]
[*Drumming*]
[*Lànké comes out, dressed as a bird.*]

SOMEONE: Ah . . .! Come out!

[*The people come out.*]

Come and look at a bird, come and look at a bird!
Come and look at a strange bird!
What sort of bird is this?
It is more beautiful than the owl!

ALL: It only resembles it,
     It is not an owl.
     It must be a water-bird!
     Its head is like the dove's
     And its colour is like the pigeon's.
     Its feathers are like a sea-bird's.
     It is beautiful!
     It is very beautiful!
     It is cool and fresh!

MAN: My wife,
What sort of mistake is this?
Instead of the bell I asked that drunkard to go and
bring for us . . .

MAN AND WIFE: We should have asked him to tell us the
name of this strange bird!

[*Bird call. Lànké flies away like a bird.*]

ALL: Ah. . . .! It is going, it is going, it is going!
Look at how it is flying away.
It is elegant!
Since we came into the world,
We have never seen a bird like this!
This bird is really strange!
If we are not to be contemptuous and even if we are,
This sort of thing is strange to us!
Its head is like the dove's
And its colour is like the pigeon's!
Its feathers are like a sea-bird's.
It is beautiful!

[*Drumming louder*]

It is very beautiful!
It is cool and fresh!

[*As they are leaving*]

MAN: This drunkard even wants to spoil our enjoyment
again!

WIFE: Not at all . . . he doesn't spoil our enjoyment!
Look! Don't you know he is entertaining us the way he
is behaving?

[*Lànké enters, carrying a bell. He is dancing.*]

MAN: [*Looking at Lànkè with astonishment. He takes the bell
fearful.*]
Ah . . .! Does it mean that you are the father of the
gods,
Truly?!

LÀNKÉ: It is so!

MAN: Who can do anything in life!

LÀNKÉ: . . . . . . . . in life.

MAN: You have tried!
But before I show you where your palmwine tapper is,
You must do something else for me!

[*To his wife*]

What *should* he do now?

WIFE: How about Death?

LÀNKÉ: Death?!

WIFE: Go and bring Death in a net
And carry him here.

LÀŃKÉ: Ah . . .! I should bring Death in a net?

[*General laughter*]

MAN: Yes.

LÀŃKÉ: I should carry him here?

WIFE: Aren't you Father-of-the-gods
Who can do anything in life?

[*Husband and wife laugh*]

MAN AND WIFE: [*Laughing*] Father-of-the-gods,
This is certainly too much!

[*General laughter*]

LÀŃKÉ: [*Facing the audience*] How is one to get to the house
of Death?
How can one tie up Death in a net?
There is no other way,
One must use one's senses.
Because the blacksmith must not say that
Iron is impossible to forge.
A potter must not say that a piece of clay
Is impossible to make a pot with.
A thing which has no mouth to talk with
Ought not be wiser than a person.

[*A young man in gay clothes is passing by.*]

Ah! . . . You . . . you . . . are welcome, friend.

Ah! You are welcome.
Please, er . . . er . . . I am asking for the road to the
house of Death:
The way we pass to the house of Death.

[*Laughter*]
[*The country fellow looks about and runs away.*]
[*Lànké lies on the ground. Two young men enter. (V.O.)*]

1ST PERSON: Ah! And a human being is the mother of this
man
Who is lying on this road!

2ND PERSON: So, he is a human being?

1ST PERSON: He is a human being!

2ND PERSON: Ah!

1ST PERSON: And he does not know that it is in the direction
of the house of Death.
That he is pointing his head.

2ND PERSON: Ah, yes! It is in the direction of the house of
Death, indeed!

1ST PERSON: Surely, it is here that he will meet Death.

[*The two of them go out. Wórò music. Lànké stands up
joyfully.*]

LÀNKÉ: [*Singing*] Ah . . . .! Ah ha!
I know the house of Death with wisdom,

I have known the house of Death with intelligence,
I shall go straight to the house of Death,
Whether he likes it or not, I will catch him with a net.
If the touraco is the owner of the blue dye,
If the àlùkò is the owner of camwood,
If the cattle-egret is the owner of [palmwine] lime,
Whether he likes it or not, I will catch him with a net.
I know the house of Death with wisdom,
I have known the house of Death with intelligence,
I shall go straight to the house of Death.


CHORUS: Whether he likes it or not, you will catch him with
    a net.
    If the touraco is the owner of the blue dye,

[*Applause*]

If the àlùkò is the owner of camwood,
If the cattle-egret is the owner of lime,
Whether he likes it or not, you will catch him with a
    net.
You will conquer them!
You will conquer them!
You will conquer them!
You will conquer them!
The leaf of the fig tree overcomes [the leaf of] the
    orange tree.
You will conquer them!

[*Lánkè comes out and starts to beat the drum which Death
hung on a tree.*]

DEATH: Who is that?
   Who is that?!
   Are you a spirit or a human being?

LÀŃKÉ: It is a human being!

DEATH: Know quite well that the drum which you are
      beating
   Will be the death of you.

LÀŃKÉ: It is what we say to the ogbó tree that it hears
      [does],
   It is what we say to the ogbà tree that it accepts.
   Whatever I tell you, Death, on this day
   Is what you must accept, because of the feathers of the
      asa fowl.
   No one kills the asa fowl,
   No one catches the asa fowl [and puts it in a coop],
   No one uses the feathers of the asa fowl for cleaning
      the ear.
   Truly, the snail has no hands,
   The snail has no legs.
   Gently, gently, the snail reaches the tree top.
   Gently, gently!
   Gently, gently, the snail gets to the tree top.

   [*Laughter*]
   [*Death does not talk (does not resist) all the time Lànké is
   tying him up in the net.*]

MAN: [*In spirit language—(V.O.)*] Do you think that
   That drunkard can ever come back?

90

WIFE: [I think so] I don't think so, because there is no one
Who can do what we asked him to do.

[*Laughter. Lànké enters.*]

MAN AND WIFE: Father-of-the-gods, where is Death?

LÀŃKÉ: Here he is.

MAN AND WIFE: Ah!

[*Lànké removes the net and Death begins to chase the man and his wife.*]

[*Laughter*]

MAN AND WIFE: This is Death! Save me!!
This is Death . . . . .!

LÀŃKÉ: Where is my wine-tapper?

MAN AND WIFE: This is Death! Save me!!

[*They run out. (V.O.)*]

LÀŃKÉ: They have gone!
They did not show me the way to the house of my
wine-tapper!

[*Blackout*]

# Woyengi

## OBOTUNDE IJIMERE

### (Excerpt)

### CHARACTERS

WOYENGI, *the great mother; goddess of creation*
OGBOINBA, *a childless woman, in possession of magic powers*
LAKPE, *her friend, mother of many children*
ISEMBI, *the king of the forest*
OLOKUN, *the king of the sea*
COCK, *ruler of 'the last kingdom of things that die'*
CREATURES *of Woyengi*
SWORDBEARERS
SPIRIT POWERS

### SCENE I

*Heaven. The stage is bare, except for a platform and a huge sun, suspended high.* WOYENGI, *the great mother, is seated on a raised platform surrounded by* SWORDBEARERS. *Before her crouches a figure completely muffled in a brown cloth—symbolizing a lump of clay about to be moulded into human form by the creator goddess. To* WOYENGI's *right stand about a dozen figures clad in white togas. They are newly created human beings, who are waiting to choose their sex, destiny, and death from* WOYENGI *before going into the world.*

SWORDBEARERS: Woyengi,
    Mother of the world,
    You are bright and radiant like the sun
    When it rises in the east.
    Your feet walk the earth
    While your head towers in the sky.
    You command the sun and the moon
    You created the earth
    When you were lonely.
    You made thousands of creatures
    From your single form.
    You create the child
    In the mother's womb.
    You make the seed flow in man
    And the blood in woman.
    You nurse the child in the womb
    You give it breath
    You open its mouth
    On the day of its birth
    And let it speak.
    You created the Niger
    That flows to the sea in multiple streams
    You placed the other Niger in the sky
    That it may fall down and water the land.
    Woyengi,
    Mother of the world,
    Your feet walk the earth
    While your head towers in the sky.

WOYENGI *now rises to the act of creation. She approaches the crouching figure which slowly rises following* WOYENGI's *movements.* WOYENGI *pulls out a naked arm from the cloth, then another, etc., until finally the cloth falls and the new creature appears, almost naked. The* SWORDBEARERS *lead the creature away to the right and clothe it in white. The mime of creation should be accompanied by very quiet, intimate music—if possible a xylophone. This should be in sharp contrast to the brisk fanfare of the praise song that precedes it.*

WOYENGI: My creatures, approach.
    The world is waiting for you
    With forests, rivers, towns and villages.
    The heat of the sun you will feel
    And the coolness of rain.
    The land is there for you to work,
    The forest to hunt in.
    You will know the pain of birth,
    The terror of death, and the happiness of love.
    Come now and choose your fate.
    But choose wisely:
    Nobody can eat the words
    He will speak here and now.
    Once you have entered the world,
    Screaming, through your mother's womb,
    Your words will have lost the power of creation.
    But for this brief moment between creation and birth.
    You share with me the power of the word.
    Every wish you utter
    Before you wade into the world
    Through the river of life
    Must come to pass.
    Approach, then, my creatures,
    And choose your fate.
    Choose—but choose wisely:
    Whether man or woman you wish to be,
    What manner of life you wish to lead,

What to achieve on earth, how long to live—
And finally—most difficult choice of all—
You must select your death.

*The* FIRST CREATURE *approaches boldly, kneels before the throne of* WOYENGI *and speaks. All subsequent* CREATURES *utter their wishes kneeling before* WOYENGI.

FIRST CREATURE: Woyengi,
     Mother of the world,
     You are bright and radiant like the sun
     When it rises in the east.
     Receive my words,
     And bless my choice:
     Let me be born a man, a real man,
     A warrior. Let me live by the power of my arm,
     Let me conquer and win,
     Let me win fame and praise.
     Do not prolong my life into feeble old age,
     But in the prime of life
     Let me die by the sword, by which I lived.

WOYENGI: So be it.
     Arise, and take your life.

*The* FIRST CREATURE *rises and moves over to the left. While the* SECOND CREATURE *kneels before* WOYENGI, *he is being equipped by the* SWORDBEARERS *as a soldier. All the* CREATURES *are thus dressed and equipped before leaving for the world.*

SECOND CREATURE: Woyengi,
     You created the Niger,

That flows into the sea in multiple rivers
And you placed the other Niger in the sky
That it may fall down and water the land.
Mother of the world:
Receive my words and bless my choice.
Let me be born a man,
A man rooted to the soil.
Let me see the yam shoot climb up the pole
Let me see corn gleam on the cob like teeth.
Let me own the palm oil that oozes, redder than blood
From the black kernel.
Let me own the palm wine that hums,
Milky white, in the calabash.
Let me grow old, to see my children work the land
Let me have grandchildren to bury me
When I die quietly in my sleep:

WOYENGI: So be it:
    Arise and take your life.

THIRD CREATURE: Woyengi,
    Mother of the world.
    You created the sun that burns the land,
    That sits on man's brain
    And confuses him with fever.
    Woyengi,
    Mother of the world,
    You created the storm
    That floods the houses,
    Crushes the trees
    And carries away the helpless fisherman,
    And his canoe in black whirlpools.
    Woyengi,

I fear the world and what it has in store for me:
Let me but peep at it.
Let me be a girl, to grow in the protection of the home,
But end my suffering soon;
In my seventh year let me return to you.
Let the sun, that is bright and radiant like yourself
Come and sit on my brain.
Let it carry me away in a mantle of fire,
Let it redeem me with its heat,
And return me to you.

WOYENGI: So be it.
   What you have chosen must come to pass.
   Arise and take your life.

FOURTH CREATURE: Woyengi,
   Mother of the world.
   You create the son in the mother's womb.
   You make the seed flow in man,
   You make the blood flow in woman.
   You nurse the child in the womb,
   You give it breath,
   You open its mouth
   On the day of its birth
   And let it speak.
   Woyengi,
   Mother of the world—
   Let me be a mother.
   Let me be fruitful, and bear children
   One, two, six, eight—
   Let me bear children until my womb dries up.
   Let me feel their toothless gums biting my breast,
   Let me teach them to walk and to speak,

Let me live to see them bear children
In their turn.
Let me die suddenly
And with joy in my heart.
Woyengi,
Mother of the world—
Let me have children;
Give them breath,
Open their mouths on the day of birth
And let them speak.

WOYENGI: So be it.
Arise and take your life.

FIFTH CREATURE: Woyengi,
You who command the sun and the moon.
You who make the sap flow in the leaves,
You who gave poison to the puff-adder,
And healing power to the ginger-lily,
Let me have power!
Let me share your secrets.
Let me be a woman—but let my womb be dry.
Little I care for children or wealth.
Let me learn the secrets of herbs and leaves;
Teach me the language of the coockal and the hornbill.
Let me have power to heal and to kill.
Give me command over the word,
Let me mould the lives of men in my hand.
Woyengi,
You who gave poison to the puff-adder
And healing power to the ginger-lily,
Let me command the spirit,
Let me be second only to you—

And let me die,
When my heart bursts with power.

WOYENGI: Bold is your wish:
  Unheard of your desire.
  Yet so be it.
  Arise and take your life.
  But when you wade into the world
  You shall not follow your fellow creatures
  Through the muddy river of happiness and wealth.
  You alone shall walk through the clear waters
  Of the spirit. Your road shall be lonely and cold—
  But your wish shall be fulfilled.

SWORDBEARERS: Woyengi,
  Mother of the world.
  The world lies in your hand,
  As you have made it,
  When you were lonely.
  You made thousands of creatures
  From your single being.
  You give them breath,
  You open their mouths
  And let them speak.
  Woyengi,
  Mother of the world:
  You alone make the sun rise in the east
  Make the seed swell in the womb,
  Woyengi, bright and radiant like the sun.

CURTAIN

100

# SCENE VI

*Heaven.*
WOYENGI *sits on the throne, as in scene one.* SWORDBEARERS
*and* CREATURES *stand by her side as before.*

WOYENGI: My creatures approach:
    The world is waiting for you!
    Come now and choose your lives,
    But choose wisely.
    Nobody can eat the words
    He will speak here and now.
    Approach then my creatures
    And choose your fate:
    Whether man or woman you wish to be,
    What manner of life you wish to lead,
    What to achieve on earth, how long to live—
    And finally—most difficult choice of all—
    You must select your death.

*The first* CREATURE *steps forwards and kneels. But before he
can speak* OGBOINBA *rushes on to the stage, followed by her
eight powers.*

OGBOINBA: Stop! Hold your words!
    Woyengi, I have conquered the world!
    The impossible have I achieved:
    'The last kingdom of those who die'
    I left behind—the first of all mortal beings
    To cross the great threshold alive.
    Woyengi, now beware!
    The powers you allowed me
    Were too great for yonder world!

They nearly burst my heart—
They split my head!
So here I am to challenge you in heaven:
Do the impossible now,
As I have done the impossible:
Eat your words, and recreate my fate!
If you refuse,
Come let us match our powers!
I feel elated now, triumphant, and
Victorious!
All the magic of Isembi and Olokun
Yes, even the powerful charms of the Cock,
Are at my side.
Woyengi: remake my womb!
Let the seed not rot in my belly,
Let not envy eat up my heart
Let me not destroy Lakpe's children!
I will command you just this once, Woyengi,
Before all powers I renounce!
Woyengi!
Reshape my fate, my life, my womb!

WOYENGI (*trembling with rage*): Mad creature!
How dare you challenge me?
I, who made the world with my hands?
Who placed the sun in the sky
Who lets the Niger flow into the sea
And across the sky?
I, who allowed you to grow in the womb,
Who opened your mouth and allowed you to speak?
Have you forgotten
That I am the source of all powers?

*Even during these words* OGBOINBA *has been stripped of all powers. She now stands trembling and whimpering before* WOYENGI, *her hands raised in an attitude of prayer.*

You asked for more
Than any other living soul!
I granted all.
Miserable, helpless creature,
Did you really think,
The powers I lent you
Enabled you to invade heaven?
You are not fit to live!

WOYENGI *grabs one of the ceremonial swords from a* SWORDBEARER *and hurls it at* OGBOINBA. *She misses and* OGBOINBA *flees in wild terror.*

CURTAIN


# SCENE VII

*A quick succession of scenes ending with* LAKPE's *house.*

OGBOINBA *bursts in from left, runs to* LAKPE, *and hides under her wide lappa.* LAKPE *is obviously pregnant.* WOYENGI *appears from left, pursuing* OGBOINBA. *She looks around for a few seconds, then goes up to* LAKPE *and stares into her eyes.*

WOYENGI: So there you are hiding!
In a pregnant woman's eyes!
Clever you are to the last,
Knowing I will not break my own law

And hurt a pregnant woman!
Well then, so be it!
Live you in the woman's eyes.
But know that never more
Will you lead a life of your own,
Never be given another beginning.
May you lead an existence of fear
Peeping out of other people's eyes.
And may you be a warning to mankind:
When they look at each other's eyes,
They will see you staring at them
And remember your mad adventure.
Never more shall man be so bold!

WOYENGI *turns to go off centre and the lights fade out on her.
As* LAKPE *and the children look after her, the rest of the cast
gradually crowd on the stage. As* WOYENGI *disappears in the
background, the huge sun from Scene I slowly descends and the
crowd fall on their knees.*

CHORUS: Woyengi,
Mother of the world,
The world lies in your hand,
As it was on the day you made it
In your loneliness.
You command the sun and the moon.
You made thousands of creatures
From your single form.
You create the child in the womb,
Made the seed flow in man
And the blood flow in woman.
Woyengi, mother of the world,
Your feet walk the earth,
While your head towers in the sky.

CURTAIN

# Index

# Bibliography

Armstrong, Robert Plant, *The Affecting Presence*, Illinois: University of Illinois Press, 1971

Dorson, Richard M., Ed., *African Folklore*, Garden City, New York: Anchor Books, 1972

Duerden, Dennis and Cosmo Pieterse, Eds., *African Writers Talking*, London: Heinemann, 1972

Goody, Jack, *Death, Property and the Ancestors*, London: Tavistock Publishers, 1962

Herskovits, Melville J., *Cultural Anthropology*, New York: Alfred Knopf, 1960

Hughes, Langston, *An African Treasury*, New York: Pyramid Books, 1961

King, Bruce, Ed., *Introduction to Nigerian Literature*, New York: Africana Publishing Corporation, 1972

Litto, Frederic M., Ed., *Plays From Black Africa*, New York: Hill & Wang

Okpaku, Joseph, Ed., *New African Literature and the Arts*, New York: Thomas Y. Crowell & The Third Press

Paricsy, Pal, *The History of West African Theatre*, Studies in Black African Literature; Budapest: Center of Afro-Asian Research, Hungarian Academy of Sciences

Pieterse, Cosmo, Ed., *Ten One-Act Plays*, London: Heinemann Educational Books

Ramsaran, J. A., *New Approaches to African Literature*, Ibadan: University Press, 1970

Roscoe, Adrian A., *Mother Is Gold*, Cambridge: University Press, 1971

Tibble, Anne, Ed., *African English Literature*, New York: October House, Inc., 1965

Traoré, Bakary, *The Black African Theatre and Its Social Functions*, Ibadan: University Press, 1972

Periodicals

*Africa*, International African Institute, 210 High Holborn, London W.C. 1V 7BW

*African Arts*, African Studies Department, University of California, Los Angeles 90024

*Afro-Asian Theatre Bulletin*, International Theater Studies Center, University of Kansas, Lawrence

*Black Orpheus*, Mbari Ibadan by Daily Times of Nigeria, Ltd., 3 Kakawa Street, Lagos

*Bulletin of Black Theatre*, American Theatre Association, Inc., 1317 F Street, N.W., Washington, D. C. 20004

*Busara*, published for Department of English, University College Nairobi, by East African Publishing House

*Cahiers d'Études Africaines*, Mouton & Co., Paris

*Cultural Events in Africa*, African Studies Center, University of Cambridge, Cambridge CB3 9DA

*Journal of Asian & African Studies*, Department of Sociology & Anthropology, York University, Toronto 12

*Journal of Commonwealth Literature*, University of Leeds

*ODU*, The Caxton Press, Ibadan, Nigeria

*Okike*, Africana Publishing Company, New York

*Okyeame*, The Writers Workshop, Institute of African Studies, University of Ghana, Legon

*West Africa*, 79 Camden Road, London N.W.1 9N1